WITHDRAWN

PLYMOUTH PUBLIC LIBRARY
201 N. CENTER ST.
PLYMOUTH, IN 46563

Spices

Edited by Rebecca Stefoff

Text © 1994 by Garrett Educational Corporation

First Published in the United States in 1994
by Garrett Educational Corporation,
130 East 13th Street, Ada, Oklahoma 74820.

First Published in 1991 by A & C Black Publishers Limited
with the title Spices, © 1991 A & C Black Publishers Ltd.

All rights reserved including the right of reproduction in whole or in part
in any form without the prior written permission of the publisher.

Manufactured in the United States of America

Library of Congress Cataloging-in-Publication Data

Wilsher, Jane.
    Spices / Jane Wilsher.
       p.   cm.—(Threads)
    Includes index.
    ISBN 1-56074-062-0
    1. Spices—Juvenile literature. [1. Spices.] I. Title. II. Series.
TX406.W55   1994
641.3'383—dc20   94-19347
                                                              CIP
                                                               AC

Spices

Jane Wilsher
Photographs by Ed Barber

Contents

Spices in our food   2
What are spices?   4
Looking at spices   6
Where do spices grow?   7
Farming spices   8
Grinding spices   12
Heating spices   13
Cooking with spices   14
Spices for medicine   16
Spices for dyeing   17
Spices for perfume   18
The history of spices   20
The gingerbread man   22
More things to do   25
Index   25

GEC GARRETT EDUCATIONAL CORPORATION

Spices in our food

Do you like tomato ketchup on your french fries or mustard on your hot dog? Mustard and ketchup contain spices, like the ones in this picture. Spices add flavor to many kinds of food.

What other spicy food do you like?

What are spices?

Spices come from plants and trees, most of which grow in tropical countries. Spices can be berries, buds, pods, bark, seeds, or roots.

Most of the spices we buy have been dried and ground to a fine powder. This makes it impossible to tell which part of a plant they come from.

Here are some spices which haven't been ground up. They are called whole spices.

Black peppercorns are berries ▶ that are picked before they ripen and then dried. White peppercorns are the ripe berries that have been soaked and had their husks removed. Look at some black and some white peppercorns. Can you feel the wrinkly skin on the black peppercorns?

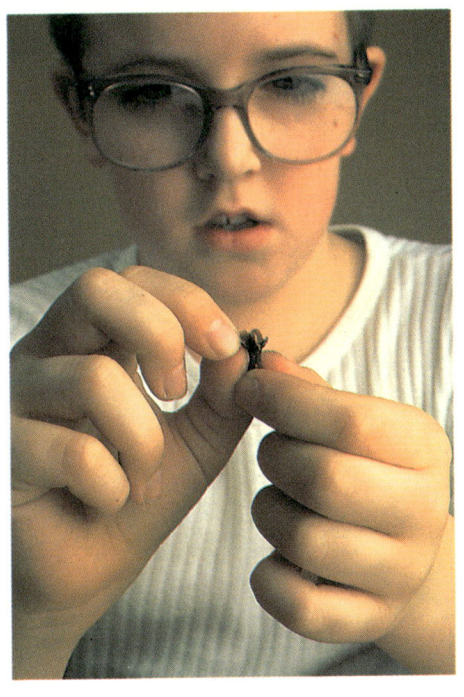  

▲ Cloves are buds that are picked before they open out into flowers. Look at a clove. Can you see the dried-up petals?

▲ Cinnamon looks and feels like wood. It is the bark from a tree that belongs to the laurel family.

▲ Peel away the green shell, or pod, from a cardamom. What's inside? Cumin, coriander, and sesame are seeds.

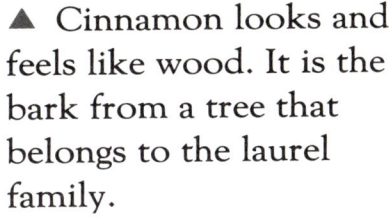

◀ Ginger and turmeric grow underground. They are roots or underground stems with shoots. Can you think of any vegetables that grow underground?

Find out which part of a plant licorice, mustard, and saffron come from.

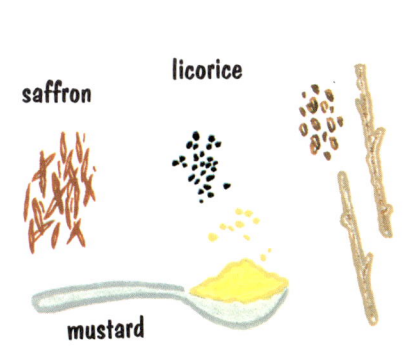

saffron licorice mustard

Looking at spices

Spices come in all sorts of shapes and colors.

Make a collection of spices from the supermarket or your local grocer's. Try to include some whole spices.

Look at each spice closely. What does it feel like? Do the spices smell the same as each other? Guess which part of the plant the whole spices come from.

Take care not to rub your eyes after touching the spices. Some spices can sting your eyes.

Did you know?

Cinnamon toast tastes delicious. Mix a pinch of cinnamon with half a teaspoon of sugar and sprinkle on hot buttered toast.

Where do spices grow?

Most spices grow in tropical countries near the equator, where the climate is very hot and wet. The equator is an imaginary line which runs around the center of the Earth.

Most of the spices we buy come from India, China, the East Indies, the West Indies, Central America, and East Africa. Find these places on a map and pin on weather symbols for hot, wet weather. Also, find the equator and mark it clearly with a piece of string or ribbon.

Look on the labels of spice jars to see where different spices come from. Record your findings on the map.

Farming spices

Each spice is grown on a separate plantation or small farm. Many countries grow far more spices than they use, so that they can sell them to cooler countries where spices don't grow.

Black pepper

Pepper vines grow on the foothills of mountains, where it rains a lot. Vines can grow up to 35 feet high. They are trained around tall trees that have few branches, apart from a shady canopy at the top. The pepper berries grow on stalks and look like tiny bunches of grapes.

In the spring, the pepper crop is harvested. Spice workers rest bamboo poles against the trees and climb up to reach the stalks of pepper, which are high up on the vines. They collect the stalks in baskets. Later, the berries are stripped from the stalks. The green berries look like shelled peas. They are spread out on mats to dry. Gradually, the berries shrivel and change color from green to black. Dried berries are known as peppercorns. They are sifted through large net trays to separate the bigger, first-quality peppercorns from the smaller, second-quality peppercorns.

Did you know?

If all the pepperconrs grown in a year were strung together, they would stretch up to the moon and back to Earth five times.

Ginger

Ginger plants grow up to 3 feet high. Six months after planting, the roots of the plant are big enough to be dug up. The roots are called hands because they look like knobbly knuckles and fingers. They are washed and their thin skins scraped away to keep them from going bad. Then they are left outside to dry.

Nutmeg

The nutmeg fruit grows on an evergreen tree. It looks like a peach and when it is ripe, it splits open like a horse chestnut and falls from the tree. Inside, bright red netting, called mace, covers the nutmeg shell.

This woman is separating the mace from the nutmeg. The mace will be flattened and then left to dry for a few hours.

Did you know?

Grenada grows a lot of the world's nutmeg, and even has a nutmeg on its flag.

The nutmegs in their shells are dried on large trays for about six weeks. As they dry, the nutmeg pulls away from its shell. When the nutmeg rattles it is ready to be taken out and the shell is cracked open like a nut. The nutmegs are then graded according to size and put into bags, ready to be transported all over the world.

Cinnamon

Cinnamon trees can grow up to 35 feet high but usually they are cut back so that the bark can be harvested easily. In the rainy season, spice workers strip away the bark from the trees' branches. This is done in the morning when there is plenty of moisture in the air and the bark won't dry out too quickly. The workers cut away the outer bark and rub the inner bark to make the sap ooze out. The sap gives cinnamon its flavor and brown color. Then the pieces of bark are pressed together and rolled into quills. The best quality quills are very tightly rolled and about 3 feet long. The quills are left to dry, before being tied together in bales.

Whole spices are shipped to major ports all over the world. Then they are transported to big spice mills where they are ground into powder, ready to be used in cooking.

Grinding spices

Every spice has a very recognizable smell or aroma. When a whole spice is ground to powder, its strong aroma is released. Try grinding your own whole spices.

You will need

a pestle and mortar

a grater

a peppermill

some whole cloves, peppercorns and a nutmeg

How to do it

1. Put a few cloves into the mortar. Press the pestle down on to the cloves and twist your wrist back and forth until the cloves become powder.

2. Peppercorns can be ground quickly in a peppermill. When you turn the lid on top of the mill, the peppercorns are crushed between blades at the bottom, and ground pepper comes out.

What happens to the aroma of a whole spice when it is ground?

3. On the fine side of a grater, carefully rub a whole nutmeg up and down. Make sure you don't grate your fingers as well.

Heating spices

Do the different smells of cumin seeds, coriander seeds, and sesame seeds remind you of certain foods? Try this experiment to see what happens when you heat up these spices together.

You will need

a heavy frying pan; a wooden spoon; a few whole coriander seeds, cumin seeds and sesame seeds; a hot plate or stove

Did you know?
The saying "Open Sesame" comes from the way sesame seeds pop from their ripe pods, just like a door lock springing open.

How to do it

1. Make sure the pan is clean and dry. Be sure to get an adult's permission to use the stove. Warm the pan on a low heat for about four minutes.

2. Put the spices into the pan and stir them with a wooden spoon. When the sesame seeds are hot they pop and jump. Do the spices change color? Do they smell the same as before? Keep stirring and turn the heat off after about three minutes.

3. Let the spices cool. Find out if it's easier to grind cooked or uncooked spices.

In Indian cooking, spice mixtures such as this one are called masalas.

Cooking with spices

Do you like apple pie baked with cloves? Cloves "go with," or complement, apples, just as mustard complements a hot dog.

Some spices also complement each other. These spices are often mixed, or blended, together before they are added to food. Did you know that a fruitcake usually contains a mixture of six spices? Can you find out which spices they are? There are lots of other spice mixtures and each one has a very special taste.

In Japan, sesame seeds and salt are sprinkled on rice.

Chinese five-spice powder is added to stir-fry and sweet and sour dishes.

Pickling spices and mustard add flavor to pickled vegetables.

Allspice, chili and cinnamon are added to the Jamaican dish Jerk Pork.

Spices are full of flavor and only a small amount need be added to food. Just a sprinkling of pepper will flavor most dishes. Find out the quantities of spices used in a Christmas pudding.

Since ancient times, spices have been used to add flavor to food that has been preserved in salt, vinegar, or sugar. Many people think that the spices also help to preserve food.

Tomatoes were first preserved as ketchup in the eighteenth century in India. Try making a jar of tomato ketchup yourself.

You will need

15 oz. can of chopped tomatoes

half an onion chopped

1 clove of finely chopped garlic

a pinch of salt and pepper

1/4 cup of vinegar

a pinch each of ground ginger, cloves, nutmeg and cardamom

1/3 cup sugar

a heavy saucepan

a stove or hotplate

a wooden spoon

a clean small jam jar with a screw top lid

a circle of greaseproof paper to fit in the top of the jar

How to do it

1. On a gentle heat, cook the tomatoes, garlic, and onions for about 10 minutes. The mixture should be as thick as oatmeal.

2. Dissolve the sugar and spices in the vinegar and add to the tomatoes. Give the mixture a good stir. Cook for about 15 minutes, stirring frequently. The ketchup is ready when it looks as thick as jam. Let it cool.

3. With the help of an adult, carefully pour the ketchup into the jam jar. Then place the circle of greaseproof paper in the neck of the jar. When the ketchup is cool screw the lid on tightly.

Make up a brand name for your ketchup, decorate a label and stick it on to the jam jar.

Spices for medicine

For thousands of years, an ancient system of Hindu medicine based on spices has helped to cure the sick. The same kind of medicine is practiced today when, after a meal, people chew a mixture of spices wrapped in betel leaves. These parcels of spices are called pans and they help you to digest your food.

Hippocrates, who lived in ancient Greece, is known in Europe as the "Father of Medicine." He wrote books about how to prepare spices and make them into medicines. The ancient Chinese also used spices to treat diseases.

In the tenth century, a famous Islamic physician called Avicenna discovered how to extract oils from spices. His writings are very important to the history of both Eastern and European medicine. Later, spice merchants experimented to find out the properties of spices. The merchants became the first apothecaries, or chemists. Then, when they knew more about the human body, they became the first medical doctors.

Today, many medicines still contain spices, especially mild antiseptics, cold remedies, and cures for indigestion.

Did you know?
Oil of cloves is good for toothache, and is used to make some toothpastes.

Spices for dyeing

Turmeric and saffron are used to dye cloth and food, especially for Hindu and Buddhist celebrations.

Try making some turmeric marbled eggs.

You will need
a stove or hotplate

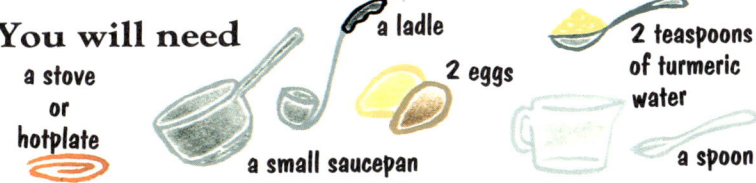

a ladle, 2 eggs, a small saucepan, 2 teaspoons of turmeric water, a spoon

Did you know?
At the Hindu festival of Diwali a saffron paste mark called a tilak is placed on a friend's forehead to wish good luck.

How to do it

1. Boil the eggs for about 8 minutes. Let the water cool and carefully remove the eggs. With the back of the spoon, gently tap and break the shells all over so they form zig-zag patterns.

2. Fill the saucepan with fresh water and add the turmeric. Put the eggs back in the saucepan to simmer for 30 minutes.

3. Leave the eggs in the water for an hour before removing the shells. Serve with salad.

Spices for perfume

For thousands of years, perfumes have been made from the sweet, fragrant aroma of spices.

The ancient Egyptians used spices to perfume and help preserve the bodies of their kings, the Pharaohs, who were embalmed as mummies.

In Roman times, oily aromatic spices called incense were burnt to ward off evil spirits. In the story of Christmas, two of the three wise men take gift of incense, frankincense and myrrh, to the baby Jesus. Today we still use incense, joss-sticks and potpourri, a scented mixture of dried flowers and spices, to perfume rooms.

Elizabethans carried fragrant pomanders, or spice balls, to protect them against disease.

Try making your own pomander.

You will need

a small orange or lemon

a pot of cloves

a length of ribbon

Did you know?

The word clove comes from the French word for nail, clou. Do you think cloves look like nails?

How to do it

1. Tie the ribbon around the orange as you would tie string around a package. Leave a loop to hang it up by.

2. Push the cloves into the orange skin so that they just touch each other. If this hurts your fingers, make holes in the orange skin with a thin knitting needle, then stick the cloves in the holes.

When the orange is covered with cloves, put it in a paper bag and leave it for two weeks in a cool dry place.

3. You can hang your pomander in a wardrobe or give it to a friend as a present. The pomander will keep its fragrance for at least a year.

The history of spices

Throughout history, spices have been in great demand because they can be used in so many different ways. Countries fought wars trying to control the trade in spices and the routes used to transport them to Europe from the tropical countries where they grow.

The Romans bought spices from Arabian merchants. The merchants could sell the spices at high prices because only they knew how to reach India where the spices grew. The merchants made up stories about the spices, saying they were found in pits protected by serpents, dragons, and a phoenix. The spices were also expensive because it took merchants up to two years to travel by land and sea from India to the markets of Europe.

Did you know?
The prophet Muhammad was a spice merchant.

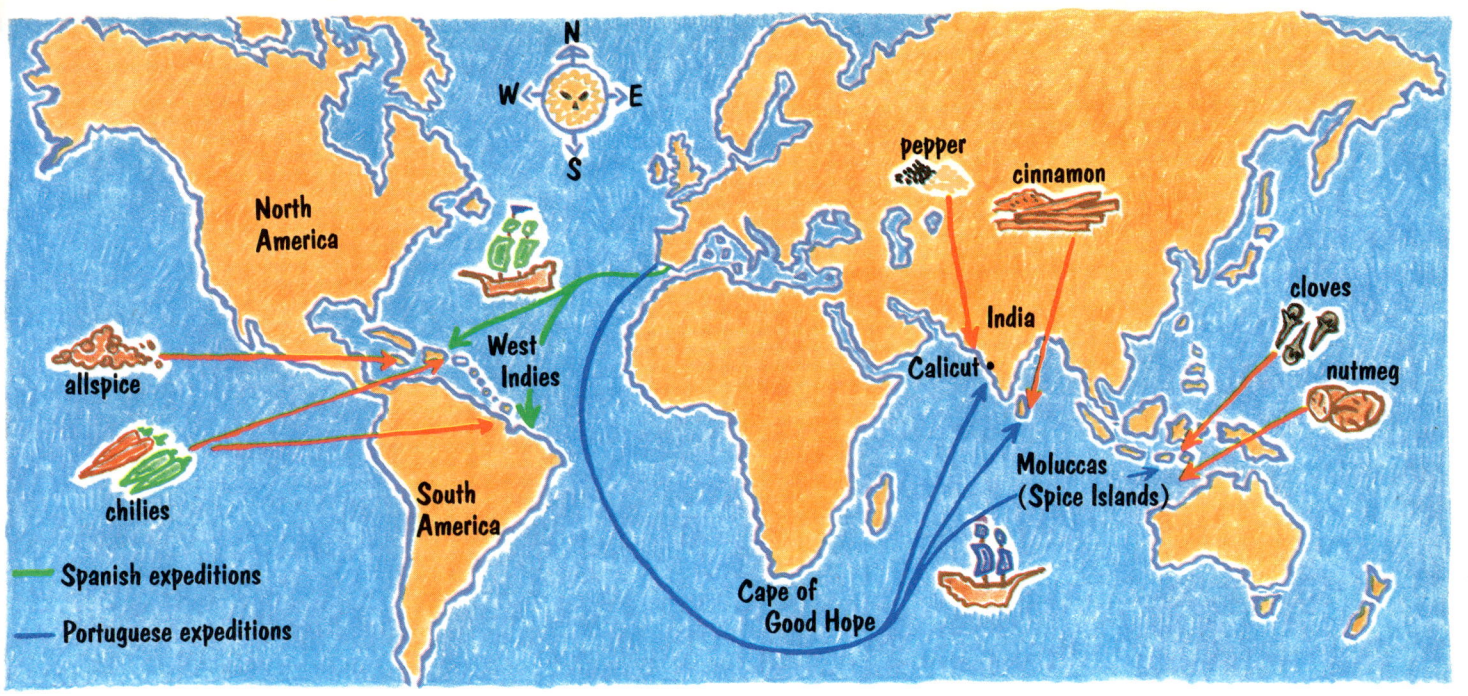

In the thirteenth century, Marco Polo, a famous Venetian explorer, returned from the East with stories of plentiful spice markets. However in Europe, spices were so rare and valuable they were used instead of money. Rents, taxes, and even marriage dowries were paid with peppercorns.

In the fifteenth century, Christopher Columbus set off from Spain, and Vasco da Gama from Portugal, in search of the countries where spices grew. They sailed long distances and discovered sea routes to America and the East. Later, their countries fought bitter wars to control the spice trade. Then, in the eighteenth century, the Dutch, and later the English, took control of the spice trade. They conquered the spice-growing lands and made them part of their empires.

The Europeans treated the spice growers badly, and it wasn't until the twentieth century that many spice-growing countries won back their independence.

The gingerbread man

Do you know the story of the gingerbread man who ran away? He sang,

Run, run, as fast as you can!
You can't catch me,
I'm the gingerbread man!

Try making some gingerbread people for yourself.

You will need

- 1-1/2 cups self rising flour
- 1/2 cup soft dark brown sugar
- 2 teaspoons ground ginger
- 1/2 teaspoon of salt
- 1/2 teaspoon of mixed spice
- 1/4 lb of soft margarine or butter
- 3 tablespoons of milk
- some raisins or chocolate drops
- a gingerbread cutter
- a mixing bowl
- a wooden spoon
- a greased baking sheet
- oven gloves
- a wire tray
- a sieve
- a rolling pin
- a rolling board
- an oven set to 400°F

How to do it

1. Sieve the flour into the bowl and add the sugar, salt, and spices. Stir the mixture.

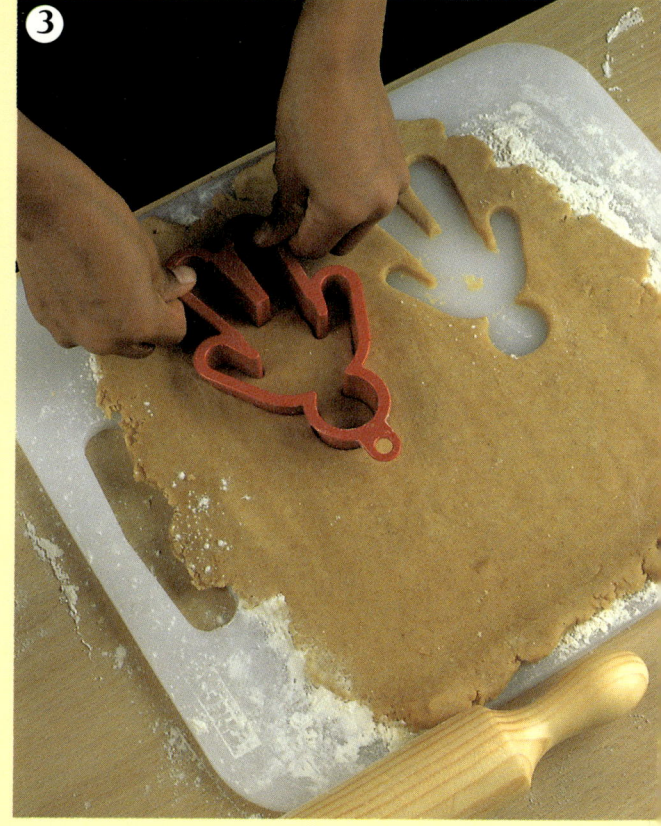

2. Cut the margarine into small cubes and add to the flour mixture. With your fingertips, rub in the margarine until it looks crumbly. Add the milk and give the mixture a good stir. It should look like uncooked pastry.

3. Sieve some flour on to the board and rolling pin. Roll out the dough to a thickness of 6 mm. Place the cutter over the dough and press to cut out a shape. Cut out as many people as you can. Carefully put them on to the baking sheet.

4. Give each gingerbread person some raisin eyes and buttons. Cook for 15 minutes. Cool the cookies on a wire tray.

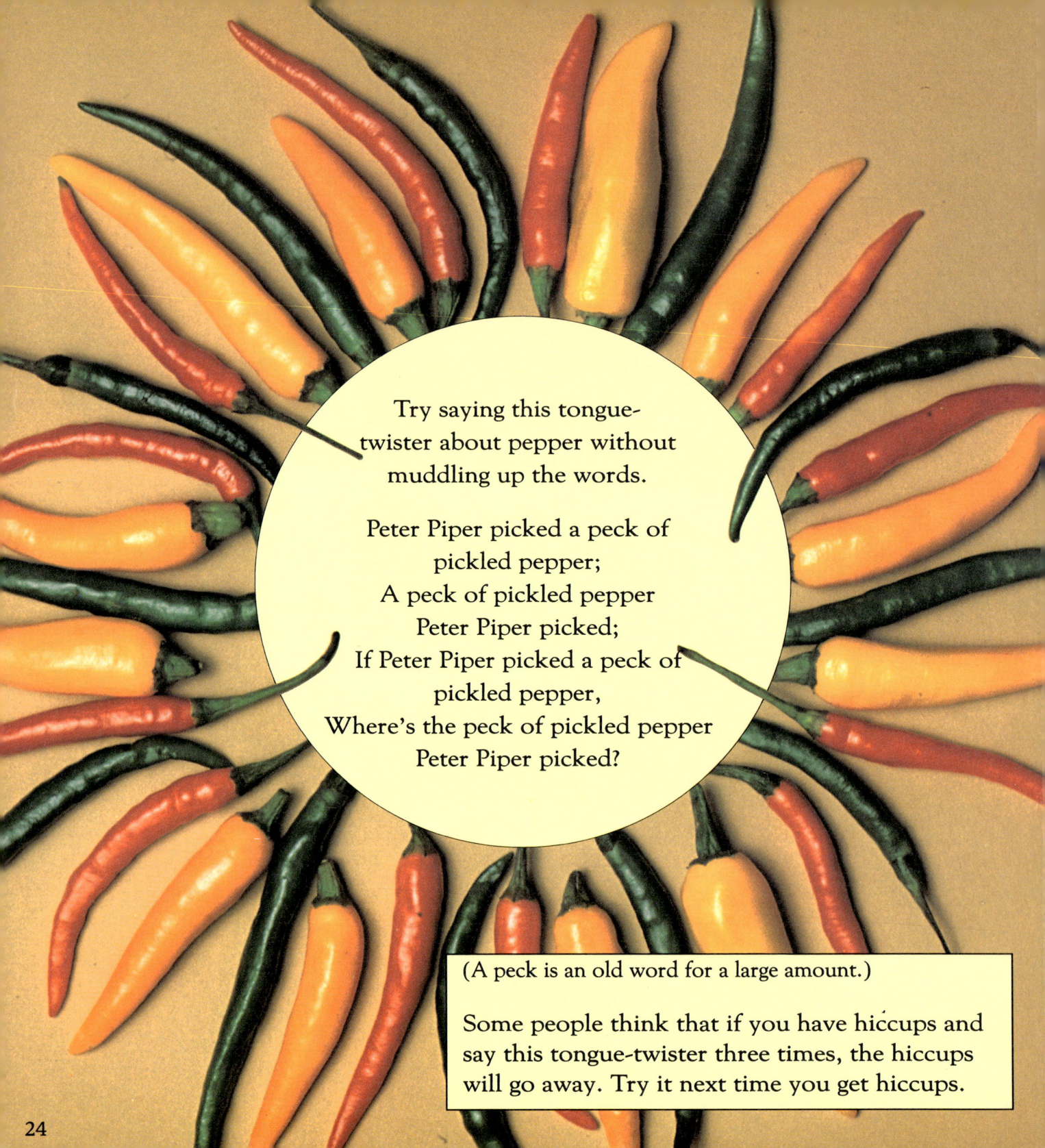

Try saying this tongue-twister about pepper without muddling up the words.

Peter Piper picked a peck of pickled pepper;
A peck of pickled pepper Peter Piper picked;
If Peter Piper picked a peck of pickled pepper,
Where's the peck of pickled pepper Peter Piper picked?

(A peck is an old word for a large amount.)

Some people think that if you have hiccups and say this tongue-twister three times, the hiccups will go away. Try it next time you get hiccups.

More things to do

1. Herbs are similar to spices, although they can grow in cooler climates. They are the leaves or stems of plants, which are used to flavor food and to make medicines. Grow and process your own herbs. Pick the leaves from mint, chive, or parsley plants, dry them in a warm place, and grind in a mortar with a pestle.

2. Look on the labels of curry powders. What spices do they contain? Can you guess which of the spices make the food taste "hot"? (See the bottom of the page for the answer.)

3. Montezuma, the Emperor of Mexico, drank hot chocolate flavored with a cinnamon stick. Try this for yourself.

4. Most of the spices we buy have been dried, but ginger can be prepared in lots of different ways. Sailors used to take pots of ginger preserved in syrup on long sea voyages. Find out all the other ways that ginger can be prepared.

5. In Mexico, coffee is flavored with cinnamon, and in Saudi Arabia with cardamom. Spices can also be added to tea. Make some masala tea. Put a cinnamon stick (or a teaspoon of ground cinnamon), 3 cloves, and 2 cardamoms into a pan with a quart of water and simmer for 5 minutes. Put two teabags into a teapot and pour in the water. Wait 5 minutes and serve.

6. Try a taste-test to see if you can taste the difference between cinnamon cookies and ginger cookies. Make a batch of ginger cookies, using the recipe on page 21. Make a batch of cinnamon cookies, using the same recipe, but substitute 2 teaspoons of cinnamon for the ginger.

7. Find out what sort of ships Christopher Columbus and Vasco da Gama sailed. In the nineteenth century, fast ships called Yankee Clippers transported spices. Find out about these ships as well.

8. A Spanish naval captain who traded in spices had a coat of arms made out of two cinnamon sticks and three nutmegs. Make your own coat of arms with whole spices.

Answer to question: Only ginger, chili, and pepper make food taste "hot."

Index

(Numbers in **bold** type are pages that show activities.)

aroma   12, 18
bark   4, 5, 11
berries   4, 8
buds   4, 5
cardamon   5, **25**
cinnamom   5, 6, 11, **25**
cloves   5, 12, 14, 16, **19**
cooking   **14-15, 22-23**
dyeing   **17**
explorers   21, **25**
farming   8-11
flavor   2, 14
ginger   5, 9, **22, 25**
gingerbread man   **22-23**
ground spices   4, 11, **12, 13, 15**
heating spices   **13**
herbs   **25**
marbled eggs   **17**
medicine   16
nutmeg   10, 12, **25**
pepper   4, 8, 9, 12, 14, **24**
peppery tongue-twister   **24**
perfume   18
pods   4, 5
pomanders   18, **19**
preserving   14, **15**
roots   4, 5, 9
seeds   4, 5, 10, **13**
spice merchants   **13**, 16, 20
spice mixtures   **13, 14**, 16
spice trade   20, 21
tomato ketchup   **15**
tropical countries   4, 7, 20
turmeric   5, **17**
whole spices   4, 6, 11

25